God Himself left Heaven and entered our world—not as a conqueror, but as a servant—to rescue us, His enemies, from death, destruction, and judgment. He did not come unaware of what awaited Him. The purpose of Jesus' ministry was not merely to teach or to heal, but to suffer and to die. From the beginning, the cross stood at the end of His path.

What the Gospels reveal is not only the violence done to Jesus but what emerged from Him under that violence. When His body was broken, when His breath failed, when pain and abandonment reached their peak, what came out of Him was not rage or bitterness. It was mercy. It was grace. It was love for others—spoken while His execution was still unfolding.

Crucifixion was designed to silence its victims, to reduce them to screams and then to nothing. Yet from the cross, Jesus spoke. Each word was costly. Each sentence was drawn out between labored breaths, through blood, thirst, and agony. These were not speeches delivered in safety, but final declarations made while dying.

His last words are preserved not as poetic sentiment but as testimony—evidence of who He was even as He was being killed:

"Father, forgive them; for they know not what they do." (Luke 23:34)

"Truly, I say to you, today you will be with me in paradise." (Luke 23:43)

"Woman, behold, your son! Behold, your mother!" (John 19:26–27)

"My God, my God, why have you forsaken me?" (Matthew 27:46; Mark 15:34)

"I thirst." (John 19:28)

"It is finished." (John 19:30)

"Father, into your hands I commit my spirit." (Luke 23:46)

THESE ARE NOT WORDS OF DEFEAT.

They are the words of a Savior who endured the full weight of crucifixion—and answered it with redemption.

after the revolt of Spartacus, a brutal reminder that every traveler would see: this is the cost of defying Rome.

WHAT IS CRUCIFIXION?

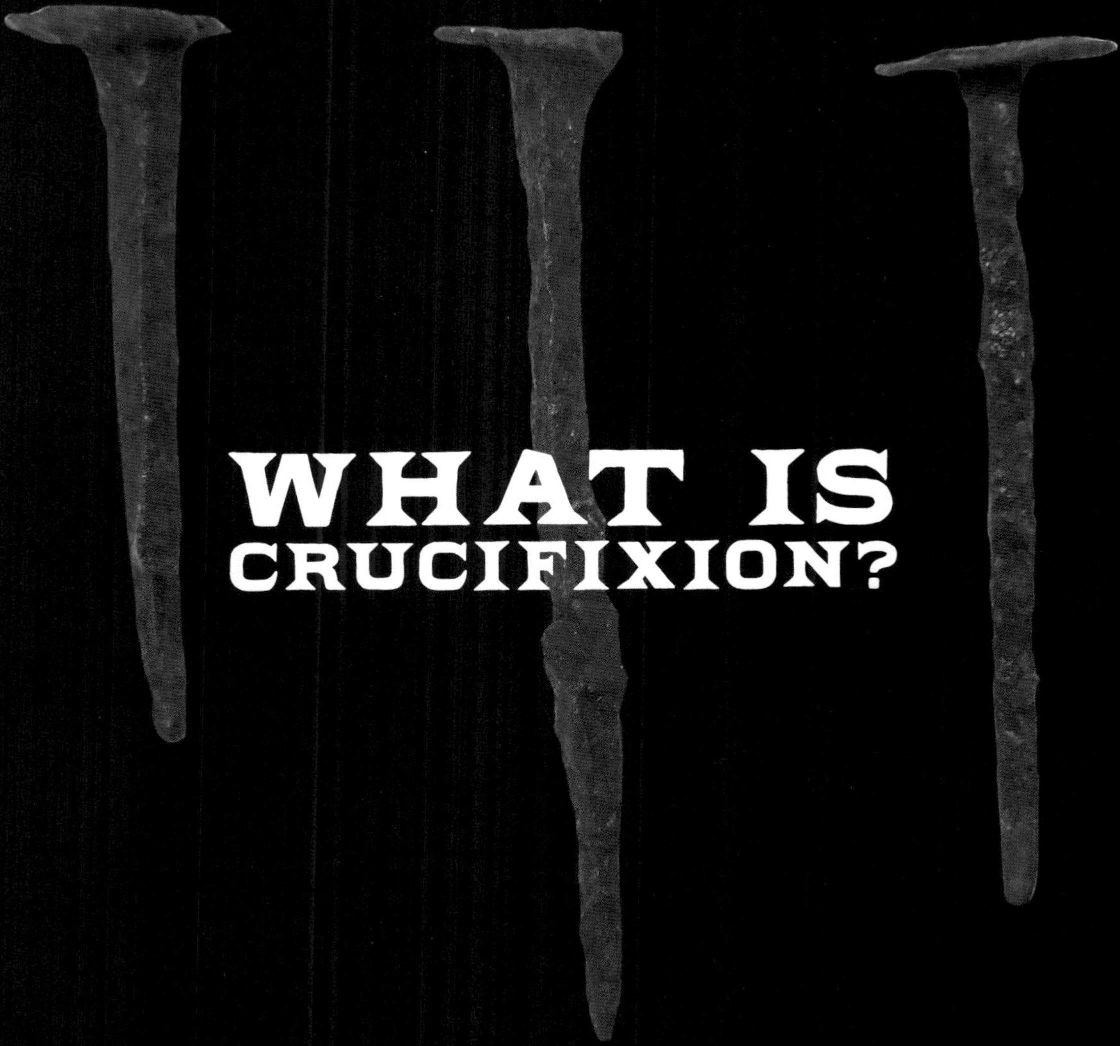

Jesus' Betrayal, Arrest, and Crucifixion

In Giambattista Tiepolo's portrayal of the crucifixion and death of Christ, an oblique viewpoint and dynamic, energetic lines intensify the scene's emotion and physical agony.

THE LAST SUPPER

At evening, Jesus sat down with the twelve to eat the Passover, fully aware that His hour had come and lovingly preparing His disciples for His coming suffering (Matt. 26:20; Mark 14:17; Luke 22:14–15; John 13:1).

GETHSEMANE

After singing a hymn, Jesus left the upper room with His disciples and went, as was His custom, to the Mount of Olives, while Judas departed into the night to carry out his betrayal (Matt. 26:30; Mark 14:26; Luke 22:39; John 13:2, 29–30).

BETRAYAL

Judas led a crowd to Jesus and identified Him with a kiss, after which Jesus was seized, bound, and led away to the high priest's household (Matt. 26:48–49; Mark 14:44–45; Luke 22:47; John 18:12–13).

DENIAL

As dawn approached, Peter denied Jesus three times, and at the crowing of the rooster he remembered Jesus' words, met the Lord's gaze, and went out weeping bitterly (Matt. 26:74–75; Mark 14:72; Luke 22:61; John 18:27).

THE CRUCIFIXION

At the third hour, about mid-morning, Jesus was crucified (Mark 15:25).

DARKNESS FALLS

From the sixth hour until the ninth hour, darkness covered the land as Jesus hung on the cross (Matt. 27:45; Mark 15:33; Luke 23:44).

LAID TO REST

As evening approached and the Sabbath drew near, Joseph of Arimathea boldly requested Jesus' body from Pilate, and Jesus was taken down and placed in a nearby tomb because of the preparation day (Matt. 27:57; Mark 15:42–43; Luke 23:54; John 19:31, 42).

FRIDAY-
THE SEALED TOMB

On the day after the preparation, the religious leaders asked Pilate to secure Jesus' tomb, fearing His disciples might claim His promised resurrection (Matt. 27:62–64).

SATURDAY-
WAITING IN SILENCE

After the Sabbath, the women prepared spices and ointments to anoint Jesus' body, having rested according to the commandment (Mark 16:1; Luke 23:56).

SUNDAY -
THE EMPTY TOMB

At dawn on the first day of the week, the women came to the tomb and found the stone rolled away, the grave empty, and Jesus risen from the dead (Matt. 28:1; Mark 16:2; Luke 24:1; John 20:1).

THE SIGN OF JONAH

Jesus declared that the only sign given would be the sign of Jonah—just as Jonah was three days and three nights in the fish, so the Son of Man would be three days and three nights in the heart of the earth (Matt. 12:38–40; 16:4; Luke 11:29).

WHERE IN THE SCRIPTURES?

Paul affirms that Christ died for our sins, was buried, and rose again on the third day, all in accordance with the Scriptures (1 Cor. 15:3–4).

FROM PASSOVER TO FIRSTFRUITS

Jesus died on Passover as the unblemished sacrifice, was buried before the Day of Preparation ended, fulfilled the sign of three days and three nights through the intervening Sabbaths, and rose on the first day of the week as the Firstfruits from the dead, inaugurating the fifty-day count.

BIBLICAL APPOINTED TIMES

The Law establishes Passover on the fourteenth day at evening, followed by the Feast of Unleavened Bread beginning with a holy convocation, and the offering of Firstfruits on the day after the Sabbath, when the first sheaf is presented before the LORD (Lev. 23:5–7, 10–11).

AN EMBLEM OF SUFFERING AND SHAME

Those words from an old hymn capture the reality of crucifixion throughout history. Long before it became bound to the story of Jesus Christ, crucifixion was engineered as an instrument of terror. It was never merely about execution; it was about domination, humiliation, and fear. From its earliest use, crucifixion was designed to be public and unforgettable.

The practice is generally traced to the Persians around 800 BC. Their method often involved impalement—driving a sharpened stake through the body and leaving the victim suspended for days, slowly dying from blood loss, dehydration, exposure, and shock. Later empires adopted and refined the practice. The Romans perfected crucifixion into a calculated system of prolonged agony, carefully positioning the body to delay death while maximizing pain. After the revolt of Spartacus in 71 BC, Rome crucified roughly 6,000 enslaved rebels along more than 120 miles of roadway. In later centuries, crucifixion reappeared wherever governments and movements sought to rule through terror—used by the Nazis, the Khmer Rouge, and modern extremist groups as a public warning meant to instill fear.

What makes the crucifixion of Jesus unique is not only its brutality but everything that preceded it. Before ever reaching the cross, Jesus endured betrayal, arrest, and hours of violent interrogation. He was beaten while blindfolded, struck repeatedly by men he could not see. He was scourged with a Roman cat o' nine tails weighted with metal and bone, tearing open His back, exposing muscle and tissue, and leaving Him weakened and bleeding before the crucifixion even began. A crown of thorns was pressed into his scalp, reopening wounds as blood ran down His face. He was forced to carry the heavy crossbeam through the narrow streets of Jerusalem until His body collapsed under the weight.

Nailed through his hands and feet, he was lifted and dropped into place, each breath becoming a struggle as his body sagged and suffocation set in. When he cried out in thirst, soldiers mocked him by raising a sponge soaked in sour wine vinegar--akin to ancient Roman toilet paper and disinfectant--to his lips. After he gave up his spirit, a Roman soldier drove a spear into his side, piercing his heart, and blood and water poured out, leaving no doubt that death had fully claimed him.

The King was dead.

Diego Velázquez's Christ Crucified strips the scene of spectacle—no crowd, no drama, only the quiet weight of the cross and the stillness of a body offered. Power here is not Rome's cruelty, but Christ's willing surrender.

1. Jesus died to take your place. There are only two options. You die and go to Hell to repay Jesus for all your sins forever, or Jesus died on the cross in your place for your sins. Sin is your biggest problem. You've sinned in your thoughts, words, and actions. You're not a good person; you're not a victim of everyone else. You're evil and a villain. You are a sinner by commission and omission. You have said and done things that should not have been said and done, and you have failed to do the things that God made you to do and to say the things that God has made you to say and believe the things that God has made you to believe and to give things that God has made you to give.

Penal Substitutionary Atonement /def/

Penal is that there's a penalty to be paid for the sin that is committed. Substitution is that Jesus dies in your place for your sins. Atonement literally means at one ment. It's bringing two people together who have been adversarial.

Tintoretto painted *Ascent to Calvary* between 1566 and 1567 for the Scuola Grande di San Rocco in Venice, where it remains part of a larger cycle of works adorning the building's walls and ceiling near the Church of San Rocco.

2. Jesus died to defeat Satan. When Jesus died on the cross, there was a rendering, a reckoning, in the unseen realm of all your sin. He died for that. Scholars will call this *Christus victor.* The rebellion against God started not on earth, but in Heaven; not with us, but with Satan. Satan recruited demons to join his cosmic treason, his horrific rebellion against God, the creator. Satan and the demons lost that war. They were sent down to the earth, and they sought to recruit us to join in their war against him. Every single one of us has chosen Satan's side of the war, and we have declared war on God. As a result, Satan is our king--unless you receive Jesus Christ as your only God and savior and the substitute for your sin, Satan owns you. Jesus' death conquers Satan's control of your life, pays the penalty for your sin, and transfers you from the domain of darkness to the kingdom of light, from Satan as your Lord to Jesus as your Lord. (Colossians 2:13-15)

3. Jesus died to set you free. It doesn't matter how much money you make, you cannot purchase salvation. It does not matter what kind of lavish lifestyle you enjoy. At the end of this life, that lifestyle comes to an end. Instead, you were redeemed from the empty way of life handed to you by your forefathers. And it was done with the precious blood of Christ, a lamb without blemish or defect. Scholars will call this redemption. You are a slave to sin. For some people, this is obvious. They have addictions they can't stop. They're in a self-destructive process of their own decision-making leading to their own demise. But the truth is, we're all slaves to sin. And if you disbelieve that, prove me wrong by being perfect.

The reason that you and I cannot be perfect is simple: we are slaves to sin. God sets us free from sin to worship Him. We tend to think of our freedom as freedom to sin. Instead, it's freedom from sin to worship. The prototype for redemption in the Bible is the book of Exodus. God's people were slaves. They could not free themselves. God set them free supernaturally so that they would be free to worship Him. And once you are set free, you are free from sin, death, wrath, and Hell. You're free to God, you're free to worship, and you're free to glorify the God who created you. When God frees you, He gives you new nature, desires, and identity. It's not just a better you. It's a new you, free to be all that God intends for you. (1 Peter 1:18-19)

4

4. Jesus died as your sacrifice. Scholars call Jesus' death the new covenant sacrifice. Sin causes death. That's why the Bible is such a bloody book: 450 times it mentions blood. It's a blood-soaked, blood-dripped book. In the old covenant, there was a temple with a priest who would bring a sacrifice. That sacrifice would be a substitute for your sin, and the priest would shed its blood. Because of this, there was a river of blood that flowed from the temple. Today, we have no temple, because Jesus is the presence of God on the earth. We have no priest, because Jesus is our great high priest. You do not bring a sacrifice to church, because Jesus Christ is the once-for-all sacrifice, the lamb of God who takes away the sins of the world. You will have your blood shed for your sins, or you will receive Jesus' blood shed for your sins. (Hebrews 9:11-12)

5. Jesus died to make you right with God. You're not born right with God. You need to be born again to be right with God. God rules through laws, and sin is a violation of God's law. You are not a law unto yourself. It doesn't matter what your gender, culture, nation, or candidate is. God rules as a judge and He judges justly and perfectly all people's times and places according to His Word.

There are two ways in which people pursue justification with God. The first is called works righteousness, which tells us to be a good person and do the right things. For religious people, they have traditions and rituals, silly things that they think will please God. For those who are irreligious, they have causes and justice and good works, and the right hashtags to try to pretend that they can make it right because they're good people. You're not a good person. You're a bad person. You don't get to just brag about your best day. You need to own your worst day. You don't need to just post everything you have done right. You need to stand before God and give an account for all that you have done wrong.

So, ultimately, the only way to be made right with God is not by something you have done, but by what Jesus has done. You don't make yourself right with God. He makes it right through the death of Jesus Christ, in your place for your sins. Jesus was Perfect. You are not. Jesus was punished so that He could receive condemnation and you could receive salvation. (Romans 5:15-17)

6

For our sake he made him to be sin who knew no sin, so that in him we might become the righteousness of God.
2 Corinthians 5:21

6. Jesus died to make you righteous. There are two ways in which people pursue righteousness: through doing things to earn God's favor or by thanking Jesus for doing all that is required for us to have favor with God. It's not about what you do. It's about what Jesus does. You can take all of your good deeds and hope that when you stand before God, you've been good enough, but Jesus says, "be perfect as your heavenly father is perfect." His standard is not good. It's perfect. God is perfect. Heaven is perfect. Only perfect people should be allowed before a perfect God in a perfect place. Your good deeds are not going to earn you relationship with God. Only the deeds of Jesus Christ can do that. He lived the life you have not lived. He died the death you should die. And he gives the gift you cannot earn: forgiveness of sin and eternal life. (2 Corinthians 5:21)

7. Jesus died to satisfy God's wrath. We live in a world where everyone is a victim; nobody is a villain. We all want justice, except for God's justice. We all pour out our wrath on the people and things that we're so frustrated by, but God's not allowed to pour out His wrath. Scholars use a big word called *propitiation*. The big idea is this: your sin triggers God's wrath. God is holy, you are unholy, and it would be unholy for Him not to respond in a holy way toward your sin. God's wrath comes in two forms. Number one, there is passive wrath where God lets you do whatever you want to do. Eventually it culminates in active wrath—the second kind--where God makes you pay for all you have done. Some of you are living in the path of the wrath of God. You're in danger.

There's a cup in the presence of God with your name on it, and every time you sin, that sin is accounted for in that cup. You're storing up everything for the day of judgment. When Jesus said, "take this cup from me," He knew that He was going to take a cup with your name on it, and He was going to drink every drop of the wrath of God in your place for your sins, so He's up all night. "Father, if there's another way, not my will, your will be done." Either you keep filling up that cup, and when you die, you drink every last drop of the wrath of God, or Jesus drank your cup and emptied it, enduring the wrath of God on the cross in your place for your sins. You are saved from God. You're saved by God. You're saved to God. And if you're not saved by God, to God, for God, you're not saved, you're damned. (Matthew 6:39)

A "cup of wrath" is a powerful biblical image that represents God's righteous judgment against sin—something to be drunk fully, not merely tasted, meaning judgment that is complete, unavoidable, and deserved.

8. Jesus died to make you clean. Jesus not only forgives you, He makes you clean. This is called *expiation.* When God's people in the Bible go to worship, they wear white, because they are clean. A bride wears white on her wedding day because Jesus makes her clean. Sin is depicted as defilement, uncleanness, filth, disgusting. You can hide your sin and hope God doesn't see it, but He does. You can blame someone else for your sin, but God knows you're responsible. You can make excuses about your culture or the systems or your genetics, or you can celebrate your sin. You can have pride in it. You can take it as an identity. Or you can have Jesus take your sin and your defilement and cause you to be both forgiven and clean. (1 John 1:7)

9. Jesus died to pay your debt. There's one God. If you disagree, you're wrong, and when you die and stand before Him, you'll realize it. There's one mediator between God and us: the man, Christ Jesus. We all need Jesus. Jesus is our only hope. This is what scholars call *ransom.* Every sin you commit accrues a debt to God. The question is, "Who's going to pay that debt?" Either you pay it in Hell or Jesus pays it on the cross. The debt is real; the payment is mandatory. The question is, "Who will pay?" (1 Timothy 2:5-6)

10. Jesus' resurrection is unique in history.
Christ suffered for you, leaving you an example that you should follow in His steps. Scholars call this *Christus exemplar.* Jesus is what you're supposed to look like. He's normal; you're abnormal. He's right; you're wrong. He's healthy; you're unhealthy. His life should be like your life. If at any point your life is not like His life, you're in sin. Sin is where we do not carry forth the character of Christ. So, you have two options. You can do like everyone else does: if they do evil, I do evil; if they hit me, I hit them back; if they hurt me, I'm bitter against them. Or you can do what Jesus did for you: they curse me, but I bless them; they hate me, but I love them; they sin against me, but I forgive them. Our world needs much more of this. The evolutionary myth that we're good and getting better is not true. We're bad and getting worse. The only thing we're getting better at is doing evil. (1 Peter 2:21)

For if while we were enemies we were
reconciled to God by the death of his
Son, much more, now that we are
reconciled, shall we be saved by his life.
More than that, we also rejoice in God
through our Lord Jesus Christ, through
whom we have now received
reconciliation.

ROMANS 5:10-11

11. Jesus died to reconcile you to God. You don't begin as a friend of God. You begin as an enemy of God. Some of us will look at what Jesus does and say, "I can't believe that he speaks to me this way." The question is, "what have you done for your enemy? How many enemies have you pursued? How many enemies have you adored? How many enemies have you suffered and died for?" While we were enemies, we were reconciled to God by the death of His son. Scholars call this the doctrine of *reconciliation.*

Sin here is living independently of God. Some people hate God. Some people disregard Him. God wants to be restored in relationship, and He does that through His son, Jesus Christ. There are two options. You live your whole life, you die, and you're entering into your eternal life, separated from God. No love, no grace, no mercy, no relationship. Or, in this life, which continues into the eternal life, you have reconciliation with God through Jesus Christ. I want that for you. (Romans 5:10-11)

The dove is Christian imagery because it visually communicates God's presence, purity, peace, and the work of the Holy Spirit—all rooted deeply in Scripture.

12. Jesus Died to Reveal God. This passage describes the scholarly doctrine of *revelation*. The point is this: we're blind. We don't see God. God sees us, but we don't see Him. And Jesus comes to reveal God. If you want to know what God is like, His name is Jesus Christ. If you want to know what the creator of Heaven and earth is like, His name is Jesus Christ. If you want to know what the savior of the world looks like, His name is Jesus Christ. You can live your life not seeing Jesus Christ as your only God and then die to stand before Him and realize that you were wrong, or you can receive Him as your only God and be reconciled to God in this life and in the life to come. Jesus came the first time to be punished for sin. He came in humility. Jesus is going to come again, not in humility, but in glory, not to be punished for sin, but to punish sinners.

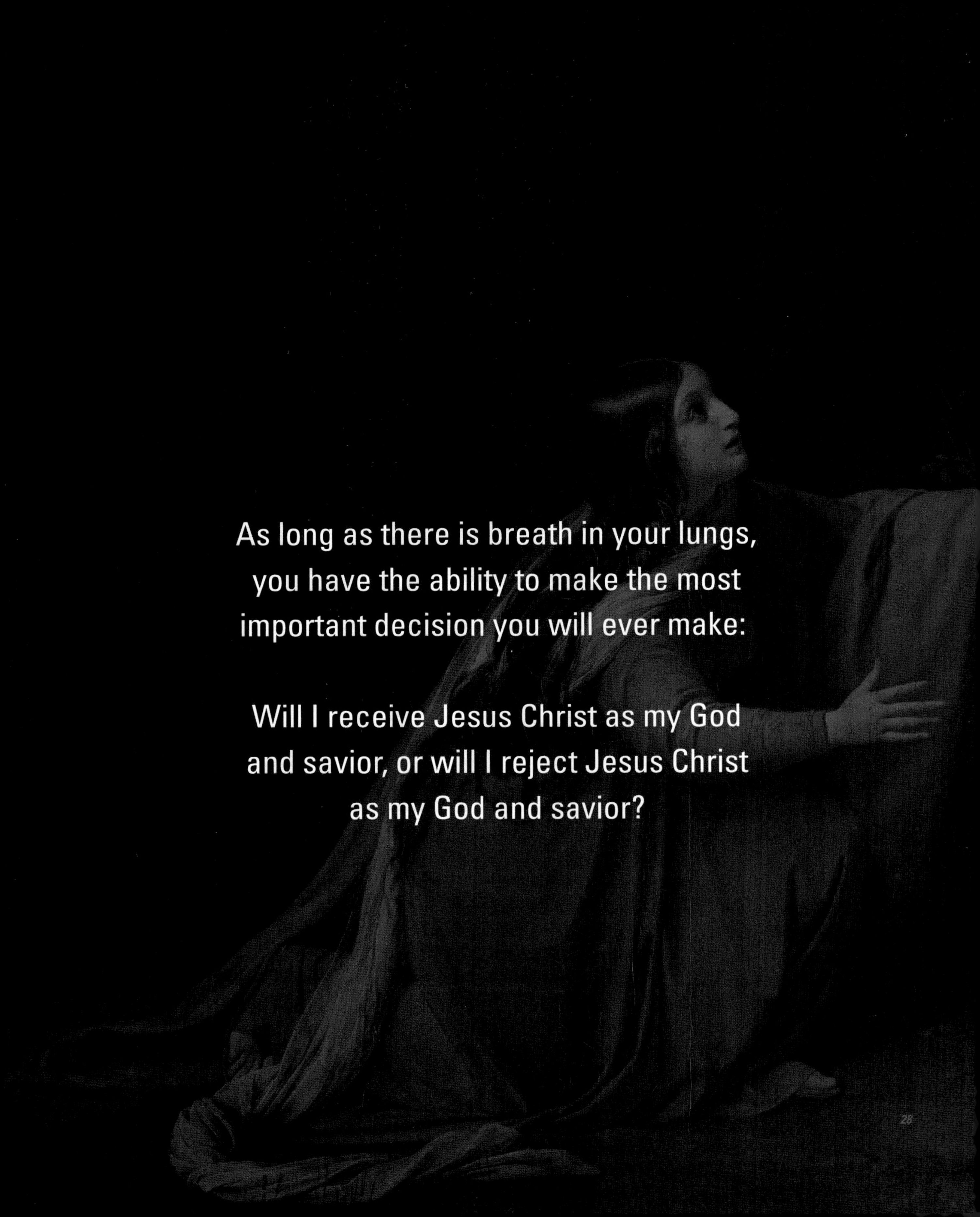

As long as there is breath in your lungs, you have the ability to make the most important decision you will ever make:

Will I receive Jesus Christ as my God and savior, or will I reject Jesus Christ as my God and savior?

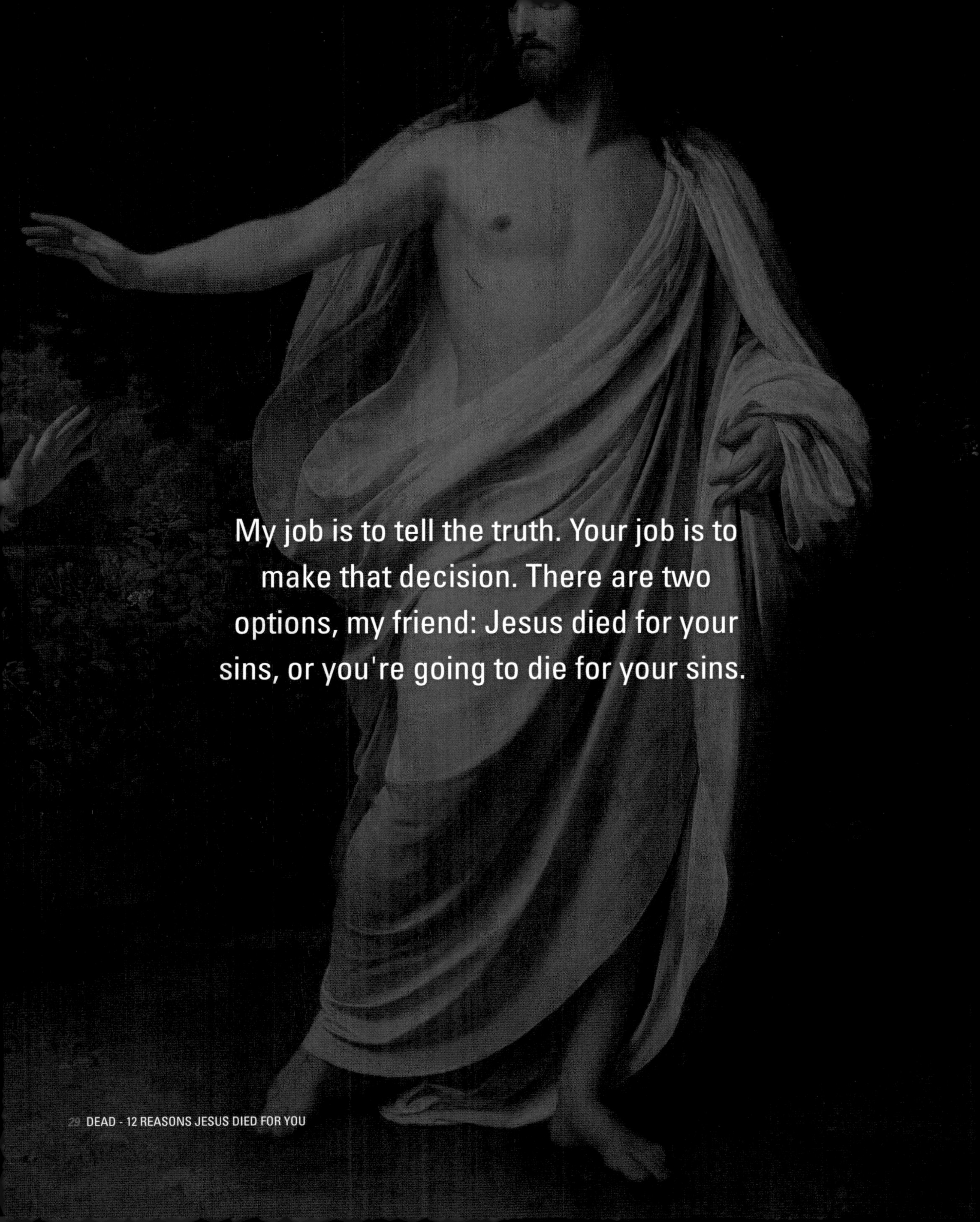

My job is to tell the truth. Your job is to make that decision. There are two options, my friend: Jesus died for your sins, or you're going to die for your sins.

Pastor Mark Driscoll is a spiritual leader, prolific author, and compelling Bible teacher. But at his core, he is a family man. Mark and his wife Grace have been married and doing vocational ministry together since 1993 and, along with their five kids, planted Trinity Church in Scottsdale, Arizona as a family ministry.

Jesus didn't faint.

He didn't survive.

He died.
For your sin.
In your place.
That's what this side of the book is about.

But if He stayed dead, none of it matters.

So flip the book.

Because the story doesn't end at a cross.

Jesus didn't stay in the grave.

He rose.
If He is alive, then death is defeated, sin is paid for, and hope is real.

But resurrection only matters because there was a real death.

So flip the book.

Because the empty tomb only makes sense after the cross.

ENDNOTES

[1] Mark Water, The Life of Jesus Made Easy, The Made Easy Series (Alresford, Hampshire: John Hunt Publishers Ltd, 2001), 35.

[2] N. T. Wright, The Resurrection of the Son of God (Minneapolis: Fortress Press, 2003), 30–31.

[3] Kenneth Scott Latourette, A History of the Expansion of Christianity, 7 vols., The First Five Centuries (New York: Harper, 1937), 1:59.

[4] James D. G. Dunn, The Christ and the Spirit (Grand Rapids, MI: Eerdmans, 1998), 67–68.

[5] Flavius Josephus, "Jewish Antiquities," in The New Complete Works of Josephus, trans. William Whiston (Grand Rapids, MI: Kregel, 1999), 18.63–64, emphasis added. There is great controversy about the authenticity of this text. Kostenberger, Andreas J.; Kellum, L. Scott; Quarles, Charles L. (2009). The Cradle, the Cross, and the Crown: An Introduction to the New Testament, pp. 104–108 is an excellent summary of the controversy.

[6] N. T. Wright, The Resurrection of the Son of God (Minneapolis: Fortress Press, 2003), 35.

[7] N. T. Wright, The Resurrection of the Son of God (Minneapolis: Fortress Press, 2003), 76.

[8] Edwin Yamauchi, "Easter: Myth, Hallucination, or History?" Christianity Today, March 15, 1974 and March 29, 1974, 4–7, 12–16.

[9] Thomas Arnold, "Christian Life, Its Hopes, Its Fears, and Its Close: Sermons Preached Mostly . . ." 15–16.

[10] C. F. D. Moule, The Phenomenon of the New Testament (London: SCM Press, 1967), 13, emphasis in original.

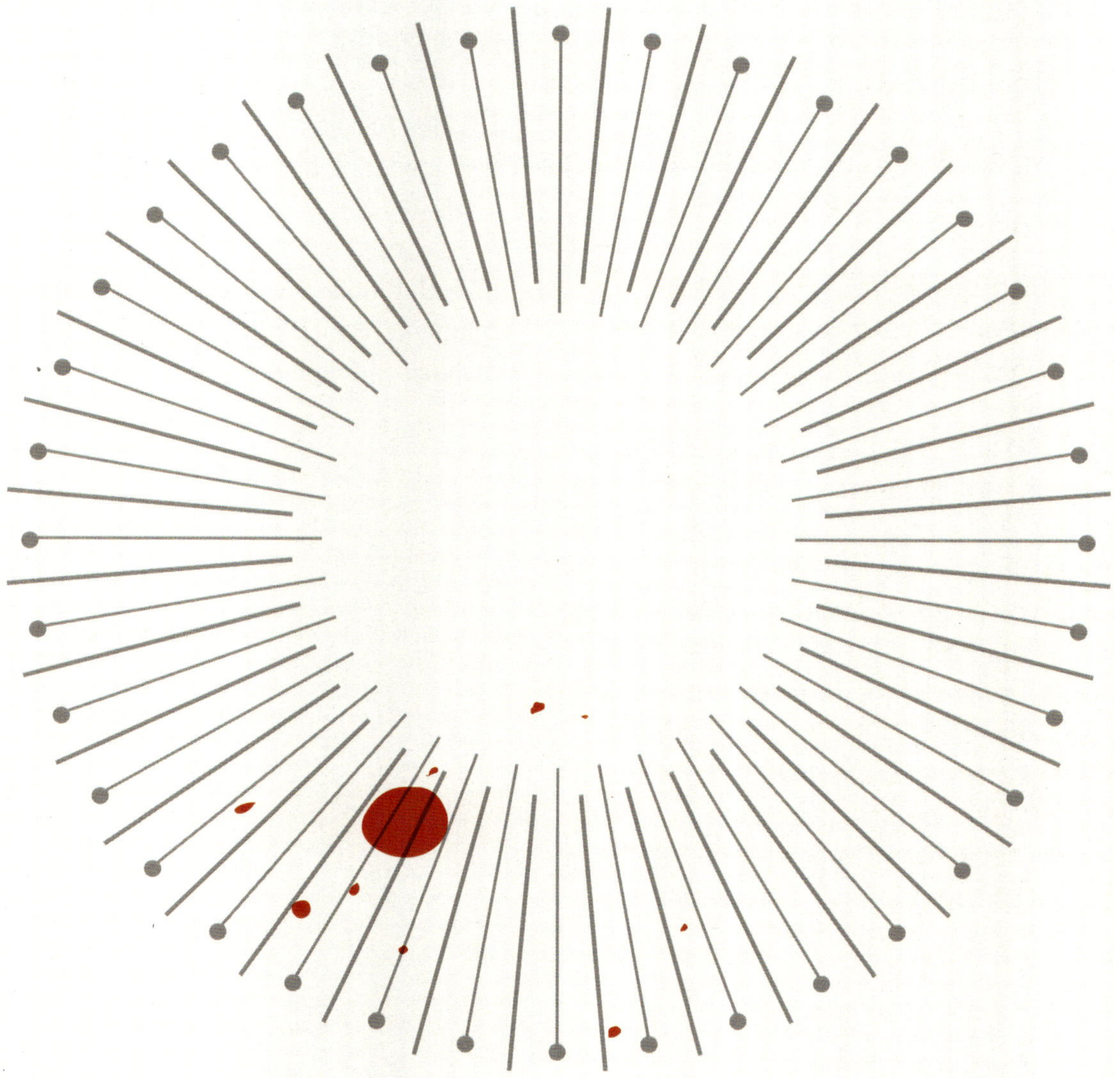

JESUS

There's no one equal to Jesus. **There is no one like Jesus.** There's no one alongside of Jesus.

Despite not having electricity, media, social media, a public relations firm, an attorney, an army, a wife, a child, money, power, or even an office, Jesus Christ is the most towering figure in all of human history. His three short years of itinerant ministry, walking around and preaching mainly to rural folks, including many illiterate peasants, without the benefit of Internet live-streaming changed the course of human history. Today, history is measured around Jesus Christ into BC (before Christ), and AD (Anno Domini, "the year of our Lord"). Non-Christian historian H. G. Wells said, "No man can write a history of the human race without giving first and foremost place to the penniless teacher of Nazareth."[1]

What did Jesus say about Himself that NO ONE else has said?

1.

Jesus said He was from Heaven and visited our planet,
"I have come down from heaven"
(John 6:38)

2.

Jesus said He alone was the One True God, and was killed for this very reason, "because you…claim to be God" (John 10:33). No other religion has its founder declaring Himself to be God.

3.

Jesus said that He alone was completely sinless, inviting anyone to disprove His perfection saying, "Which of you can truthfully accuse me of one single sin?"
(John 8:46)

4.

Jesus said that He alone could forgive sin saying, "your sins are forgiven" which puzzled the religious leaders because THE problem God has with us is sin and, "Who can forgive sins but God alone?"
(Mark 2:5, 7–8)

5.

Jesus promised to defeat death as proof that He is the only God, "he began to tell them about the terrible things he would suffer… and be killed, and that he would rise again three days afterwards."
(Mark 8:31)

6.

Jesus said He was the only way to Heaven, "I am the way and the truth and the life. No one comes to the Father except through me."
(John 14:6)

WHAT IS RESURRECTION?

The stories of near-death experiences, or of people who were pronounced dead coming back to life are revivifications, not resurrections, because those people eventually die again. Jesus' resurrection, which is the pattern for our resurrection, means to die, return from death, and defeat death to never die again, living an eternal life with your body and soul reunited forever.

In the most scholarly book ever written on resurrection, The Resurrection of the Son of God, N. T. Wright proves that in the first century, resurrection did not mean "life after death" in the sense of "the life that follows immediately after bodily death." Instead, "'Resurrection' denoted a new embodied life which would follow whatever 'life after death' there might be. 'Resurrection' was, by definition, not the existence into which someone might (or might not) go immediately upon death; it was not a disembodied 'heavenly' life; it was a further stage, out beyond all that. It was not a redescription or redefinition of death. It was death's reversal."[2]

RESURRECTION

Step 1
Living in your body with your soul.

Step 2
Die with your body in the ground and your soul with the Lord.

Step 3
Return to life with your body and soul reunited to never die again.

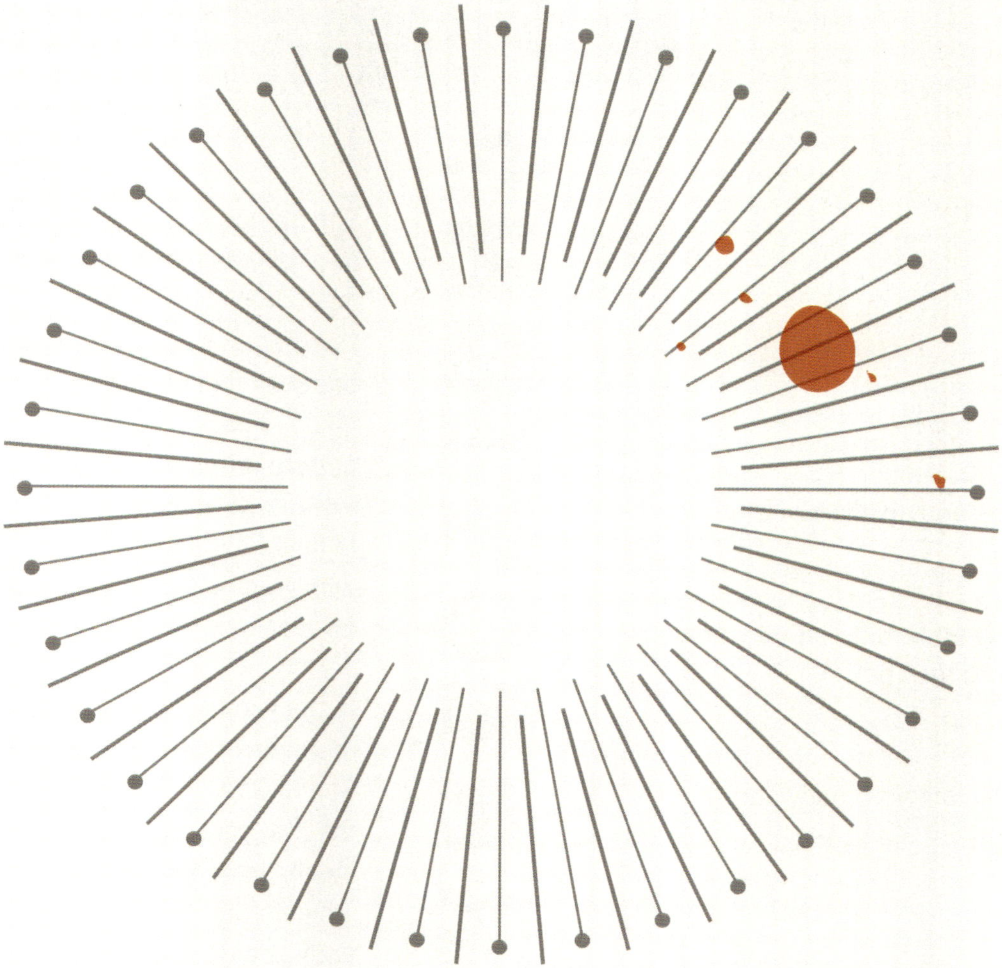

21

REASONS TO BELIEVE IN THE RESURRECTION OF JESUS CHRIST

1

1. Jesus died by execution from the ancient Roman government. After being beaten beyond recognition for an entire night, Jesus carried a heavy wooden crossbar on His bloodied back. Jesus was then nailed to a cross through the most sensitive nerve centers on the body, His hands and feet. To ensure Jesus died, a soldier took a spear, ran it under His rib cage puncturing His heart sack so that water and blood flowed from His side. Jesus was dead. Jesus' dead body was then wrapped in upwards of a hundred pounds of burial linens and spices and laid in a cold tomb hewn out of rock without any medical attention for three days.

a. "Christ died for our sins…" I Corinthians 15:3
b. What is crucifixion?

Imagine a long wooden stake being run through a person's midsection, and that stake then being driven into the ground, with the impaled person left to die slowly over the course of many days. This barbarous torture from the 9th century BC may be the earliest form of crucifixion.

The transition from impalement to crucifixion occurred under Alexander in the 4th century BC as he was a master of terror and dread. In the 1st century BC the former gladiator Spartacus fell in battle to the Romans, resulting in six thousand men being crucified along the shoulder of the highway on a single day.

The Romans perfected crucifixion, reserving it as the most painful mode of execution for the most despised people. The crucifixion methods varied with the sadism of the soldiers, as they tried to outdo one another, experimenting with torture to prolong pain and agony.

The Romans are believed to be the first to crucify on an actual cross. The Tau was a capital T cross and the Latin was a lowercase t cross. Both had the stipe (the vertical post) and patibulum (the crossbar). The stipe was probably permanent while each man carried his own patibulum.

The pain of crucifixion is so horrendous that a word was invented to explain it—excruciating—which literally means "from the cross." Crucifixion was painfully slow death by asphyxiation for the crucified, passing in and out of consciousness often for days on end.

None of this was done in privacy, but rather in public places. It would be like nailing a bloodied, naked man above the front entrance to your local mall as state sponsored terror. People were likely crucified at eye level, looking their mockers in the face as they sweated in the sun, bled, and became incontinent from the pain.

Crucifixion was the most painful and shameful way to die. God's people considered crucified people cursed, "If someone guilty of a capital offense is put to death...you must not leave the body hanging on the pole overnight...because anyone who is hung on a pole is under God's curse." (Deuteronomy 21:22–23)

The night before His crucifixion, Jesus went to the Garden of Gethsemane with His disciples to pray. His anxiety is so great that He begins to sweat as drops of blood, a medical condition called hematidrosis.

Jesus is then betrayed by Judas Iscariot, a covert pretend friend. Judas had been stealing from Jesus for years, while plotting His murder with religious and political leaders. Beaten all night, exhausted, and dehydrated, Jesus is then scourged by a flagrum (also called a cat of nine tails). It was comprised of a handle from which straps of leather would proceed, with stone or metal ball to tenderize the human flesh so that the hooks could then sink into the deep tissue, and even organs or bones, of the victim. The flesh would be repeatedly ripped off the victim's shoulders, back, buttocks, and legs—sometimes breaking a rib off the body as well—in what some doctors compare to a shotgun blast.

Jesus' bloodied and traumatized bare back and shoulders were then forced to carry His roughly hewn wooden cross to His place of crucifixion. If Jesus carried the entire cross, it would have weighed a few hundred pounds, and many think it is more likely he carried just the crossbar (patibulum), which would have been around one hundred pounds.

Despite his young age and good health, Jesus was so physically devastated from His sleepless night, miles of walking, severe beating, and scourging that He collapsed under the weight of the cross, unable to carry it alone through the narrow streets of the Old City of Jerusalem filled with shoppers.

Doctors have said that the trauma from the heavy crossbar crushing His chest into the ground could have caused a bruised heart, similar to the chest trauma caused by a car accident without a seatbelt where the driver is violently thrown against the steering wheel.

Unable to continue carrying His cross on the roughly one-mile journey to His execution, Simon of Cyrene was appointed to help carry Jesus' cross. Upon arriving at His place of crucifixion, they pulled Jesus' beard out—an act of ultimate disrespect in ancient cultures—spat on Him, and mocked Him in front of His family and friends.

"...if Christ has not been raised, then your faith is useless and you are still guilty of your sins."
1 Corinthians 15:17

A crown of thorns was then placed on Jesus' head to mock Him as King of Kings and Lord of Lords. A painting later discovered from a second-century Roman graffito depicts the head of a donkey being crucified, with a man standing alongside it with his arms raised. The caption reads, "Alexamenos worships his god" which summarizes what people thought about Christ and Christians.

To silence Jesus on the cross, a Roman soldier took a sponge, placed it on the end of a stick, sopped it in sour wine, and shoved it in His mouth. It was likely part of the military field kit used as toilet paper and disinfectant while in the field of battle. Jesus died praying for people while tasting the bowel movement of His killer. Jesus then breathed His last and died crying out, "It is finished."

To ensure Jesus was dead, a military executioner ran a spear through Jesus' side, which punctured His heart sac, and water and blood flowed from His side. This is evidence that Jesus died of a heart attack; the sac around the heart filled with water until the pressure caused Jesus' heart to stop beating. Jesus died with both a literal and metaphorical broken heart. On the cross, Jesus took your place and put you in His place. He died, so that you could live. He was cursed, so you could be blessed. He was separated from the Father, so you could be reconciled to the Father. All of this was done to Jesus, but for you, "God made Christ, who never sinned, to be the offering for our sin, so that we could be made right with God through Christ" (2 Corinthians 5:21).

On the cross, Jesus took your place and put you in His place. He died, so that you could live. He was cursed, so you could be blessed. He was separated from the Father, so you could be reconciled to the Father. All of this was done to Jesus, but for you, "God made Christ, who never sinned, to be the offering for our sin, so that we could be made right with God through Christ" (2 Corinthians 5:21).

2. Jesus' resurrection was predicted in the Old Testament. 1000 B.C. Psalm 16:10 says, "...you will not abandon me to the grave, nor will you let your Holy One see decay."

700 B.C. Isaiah 53:7–11 says, "He was oppressed, and... afflicted... like a lamb that is led to the slaughter... By oppression and judgment he was taken away... he was cut off out of the land of the living, stricken for the transgression of my people... they made his grave with the wicked and with a rich man in his death... Yet it was the will of the Lord to crush him; he has put him to grief; when his soul makes an offering for guilt, he shall see his offspring; he shall prolong his days... Out of the anguish of his soul he shall see and be satisfied; by his knowledge shall the righteous one, my servant, make many to be accounted righteous, and he shall bear their iniquities."

3. Jesus predicted His resurrection in advance. Mark 9:31 "I, the Messiah, am going to be betrayed and killed and three days later I will return to life again."

Mark 10:33–34 "I, the Messiah, will be arrested and taken before the chief priests and the Jewish leaders, who will sentence me to die and hand me over to the Romans to be killed. They will mock me and spit on me and flog me with their whips and kill me; but after three days I will come back to life again."

4. Jesus' tomb location was well-known. Some 700 years before Jesus was born, God promised that Jesus would be assigned a grave "with a rich man in his death." (Isaiah 53:9) This was incredibly unlikely, because Jesus was a very poor man who could not have afforded an expensive burial plot. This prophecy was fulfilled when, "a rich man from Arimathea, named Joseph...was a disciple of Jesus...And Joseph took the body and wrapped it in a clean linen shroud and laid it in his own new tomb, which he had cut in the rock. And he rolled a great stone to the entrance of the tomb and went away" (Matthew 27:57-60). Jesus' tomb was easy to find because it belonged to a well-known affluent man who was still alive and legally owned it.

5. Jesus' tomb was guarded by the Roman government. To secure Jesus' dead body, "Pilate said... 'You have a guard of soldiers. Go, make it as secure as you can.' So they went and made the tomb secure by sealing the stone and setting a guard" (Matthew 27:65–66).

6. Jesus' empty tomb was found by women. If the historical record of the Bible were fiction and not fact, women would not have been fabricated as the first eyewitnesses to the empty tomb, because their testimony was not as credible in court. Because these women honored their Lord, the Lord honored their testimony: "on the first day of the week [Sunday], at early dawn, they went to the tomb...And they found the stone rolled away from the tomb, but when they went in they did not find the body of the Lord Jesus...it was Mary Magdalene and Joanna and Mary the mother of James and the other women with them..." (Luke 24:1–3, 10).

7. Jesus' disciples were transformed from cowards to courageous. Prior to Jesus' resurrection, His disciples were cowards with Peter denying Him, and Thomas doubting Him. Both men later died for Jesus as martyrs, along with other disciples, because they no longer feared death. John 20:24–28 reports this transformation from cowards to courageous, "Thomas, one of the twelve...was not with them when Jesus came. So the other disciples told him, 'We have seen the Lord.' But he said to them, 'Unless I see in his hands the mark of the nails, and place my finger into the mark of the nails, and place my hand into his side, I will never believe.' Eight days later...Jesus came and stood among them and said, 'Peace be with you.' Then he said to Thomas, 'Put your finger here, and see my hands; and put out your hand, and place it in my side. Do not disbelieve, but believe.' Thomas answered him, 'My Lord and my God!'".

"...you will not abandon me to the realm of the dead, nor will you let your faithful one see decay."
Psalm 16:10

8

8. After Jesus rose from death, He appeared to crowds upwards of 500 people over the course of 40 days. Jesus was available in His risen body to meet and talk with people following His resurrection, "For forty days after his death he appeared to them many times in ways that proved beyond doubt that he was alive. They saw him, and he talked with them..." (Acts 1:3).

Jesus' resurrection was so well known that large crowds came to Him after He defeated death, "I delivered to you as of first importance...Christ died for our sins in accordance with the Scriptures, that he was buried, that he was raised on the third day in accordance with the Scriptures, and that he appeared to Cephas, then to the twelve. Then he appeared to more than five hundred brothers at one time, most of whom are still alive, though some have fallen asleep [died]" (1 Corinthians 15:3–6).

9. Jesus' followers remained loyal to Him. On the day that Jesus died, three men were crucified, and two thousand years later only one has a global movement of devoted followers willing to die as martyrs. Why? Only Jesus died and then rose from death. Historian Kenneth Scott Latourette says, "It was the conviction of the resurrection of Jesus which lifted his followers out of the despair into which his death had cast them and which led to the perpetuation of the movement begun by him. But for their profound belief that the crucified had risen from the dead and that they had seen him and talked with him, the death of Jesus and even Jesus himself would probably have been all but forgotten."[3]

10. Jesus' tomb was not enshrined. When a beloved person dies, we mark their grave to honor them. When a prophet or holy person dies, a shrine is made for their followers to visit. Of the four major world religions based upon a founder, only Christianity lacks a known grave or shrine. Abraham's Jewish holy site is at Hebron. Buddha's holy site is in India. Mohammed's Islamic holy site is in Medina. Each of these graves are visited by millions of people every year. Scholars have also found the tombs of at least 50 religious leaders enshrined in Jesus' day, but no sign of Jesus' burial place. No one knows where Jesus was buried, because He's no longer dead. Instead, He walked away from His tomb. According to former professor at the University of Durham James D. G. Dunn, there is "absolutely no trace" of any veneration at Jesus' tomb.[4]

11. Jesus' followers worshiped Him as God.
The first two of the Ten Commandments are that there is only one God, and that God alone is to be worshiped. For devout Jewish worshipers to begin worshiping Jesus as the One True God was a revolutionary shift in their history. If untrue, it also meant that everyone who worshiped Jesus was doomed to hell. They believed Jesus' words that He was the God of their ancestors risen from death and spoke truth when He said, "as for the resurrection of the dead, have you not read what was said to you by God: 'I am the God of Abraham, and the God of Isaac, and the God of Jacob'? He is not God of the dead, but of the living" (Matthew 22:31–32).

12. Jesus' family worshiped Him as God.
James, Jesus' half-brother, was originally opposed to the claims of deity by his brother (John 7:5), but a transformation occurred in James after he saw his brother resurrected from death (1 Corinthians 15:7). James went on to pastor the church in Jerusalem and authored the New Testament book bearing his name. Jesus' mother Mary was part of the early church that prayed to and worshiped her son as the Son of God, along with James and Jude (Acts 1:14). Jesus' brother Jude also wrote a book of the New Testament bearing his name. It is impossible to conceive of Jesus convincing His own mother and brothers to suffer persecution in this life and choose the torments of Hell in eternal life for worshiping Him as the one true God unless He proved His deity by resurrecting from death.

"But I saw none of the other apostles except James the Lord's brother." (Galatians 1:19)

"James, a servant of God and of the Lord Jesus Christ, To the twelve tribes in the Dispersion: Greetings." (James 1:1)

"Jude, a servant of Jesus Christ and brother of James, To those who are called, beloved in God the Father and kept for Jesus Christ:" (Jude 1:1)

13

> "I am the Living One. I was dead, but look, I am alive forever. I have power over death and hell."
> Jesus Christ
> **Revelation 1:18**

13. Jesus' followers changed the Sabbath from Saturday to Sunday. The early church stopped worshiping on Saturday, as Jews had for thousands of years, and suddenly began worshiping on Sunday in memory of Jesus' Sunday resurrection (Acts 20:7; 1 Corinthians 16:1–2). The Jewish seven-day week with a Saturday Sabbath was established by God at creation. The Sabbath was so sacred to the Jews that they would not have ceased to obey one of the Ten Commandments unless Jesus had resurrected in fulfillment of their Old Testament Scriptures. Yet, by the end of the first century, Sunday was called "the Lord's Day" (Revelation 1:10). To change the Sabbath was an attempt to literally reset the entire week, change their days of work and rest, and alter the business and worship dealings of the entire nation around Jesus' resurrection.

14. Jesus' followers practiced communion and baptism. God's people welcomed the sacraments of baptism and communion into their worship of Jesus as God. In communion, the early Christians remembered Jesus' death in their place for their sins. In baptism they remembered Jesus' resurrection in their place for their salvation and anticipated their personal future resurrection. These ancient practices have continued for thousands of years wherever the Church has existed.

The Gospel of Mark; first century document thought to be among the earliest writings of the early Bible.

15. Jesus' enemy, Paul, was converted. Paul was a devout Jewish Pharisee who routinely persecuted and killed Christians (Phil. 3:4–6; Acts 7:54–60). After an encounter with the risen Christ, Paul was converted and became the most dynamic defender and expander of the church. (Acts 9). Had Jesus not truly risen from death, it is absurd to assume that Paul would ever have worshiped Him as God, particularly when Paul rightly believed that worshiping a false God would send one into the eternal flames of Hell. Paul hated Jesus and would never have changed unless Jesus had risen from death to prove Paul wrong. Furthermore, Paul insisted that Jesus had risen in almost all his New Testament letters.

The Greek cross has equilateral arms, the shape of the Greek letter chi, is an early Christian symbol.

16. Jesus' resurrection was recorded shortly after it occurred. Mark's Gospel account of the days leading up to Jesus' crucifixion mentions the high priest without naming him because he expected his readers to know who he was speaking of (14:53, 54, 60, 61, 63). Since Caiaphas was high priest from AD 18–37, the latest possible date for the mention is AD 37, which is within a few short years of Jesus' death when eyewitnesses were still alive.

Jesus' resurrection was celebrated in the earliest church creeds. In 1 Corinthians 15:3–4, Paul says, "Christ died for our sins in accordance with the Scriptures, that he was buried, that he was raised on the third day in accordance with the Scriptures." This statement is widely accepted as the earliest church creed, which began circulating as early as AD 30–36, shortly after Jesus' resurrection.

These facts prove that there was not sufficient time between the crucifixion and the report of Jesus' resurrection for a myth to become popular. In addition, the resurrection eyewitnesses were still alive and available to be questioned about the facts surrounding the resurrection.

17

17. Jesus' resurrection is unique in history.

For those who doubt or disbelieve that the Bible is historically accurate, the following quote from the ancient Jewish historian Josephus born shortly after Jesus' resurrection helps affirm it as historical fact:

> "About this time there lived Jesus, a wise man, if indeed one ought to call him a man. For he was one who wrought surprising feats and was a teacher of such people as accept the truth gladly. He won over many Jews and many of the Greeks. He was the Christ. When Pilate, upon hearing him accused by men of the highest standing amongst us, had condemned him to be crucified, those who had in the first place come to love him did not give up their affection for him. On the third day he appeared to them restored to life, for the prophets of God had prophesied these and countless other marvelous things about him. And the tribe of the Christians, so called after him, has still to this day not disappeared."[5]

A page from Josephus' Antiquities, manuscript on vellum, early 11th or early 12th century, auctioned by Sotheby's.

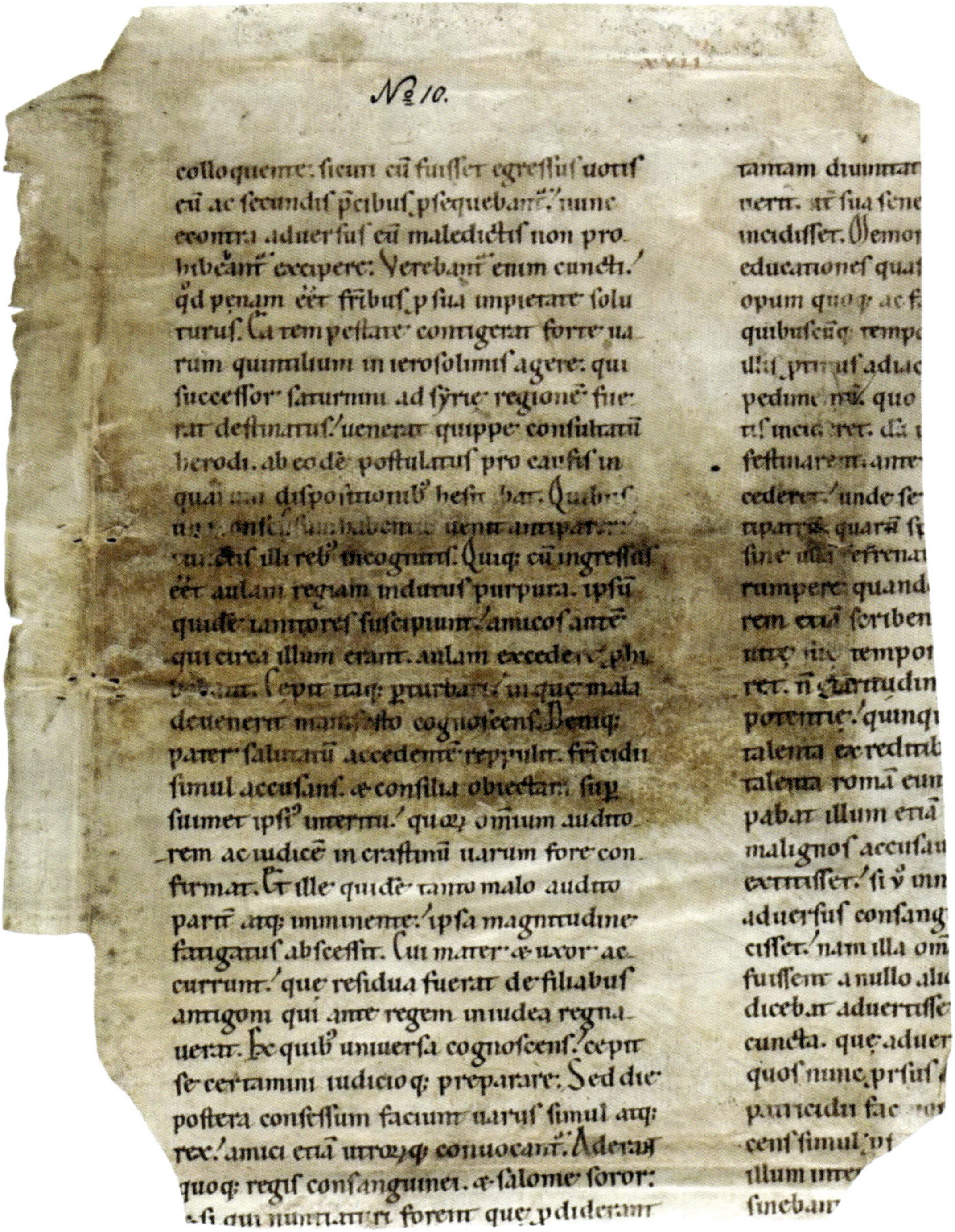

The lily is representative of Christ's resurrection. It speaks of purity and innocence, being untainted by the world. It also represents a new season, a new birth, blooming in Easter season.

The ancient Greek myth of the Phoenix tells of a bird consumed by fire, rising anew from its ashes. The resurrection of Jesus is another thing entirely.

18. There was no concept of individual resurrection prior to Jesus. The ancient Jews had a concept of all of God's people rising together at the end of history, but no concept of one person rising alone in the middle of history as Jesus did (Daniel 12:2).

In the ancient world, Greek philosophy believed the physical body was bad, but the spiritual soul was good. The goal was to die, leave the body, and live in the soul. The Greeks had no desire for a resurrection and in fact the exact opposite was true. Oxford graduate and St. Andrews professor N.T. Wright has published the most thorough academic work on the concept of resurrection throughout history. He says, "Christianity was born into a world where its central claim was known to be false. Many believed that the dead were non-existent; outside Judaism, nobody believed resurrection...."[6]

N.T. Wright continues, "Nobody in the pagan world of Jesus' day and thereafter actually claimed that somebody had been truly dead and had then come to be truly, and bodily, alive once more."[7]

Noted historian and professor Edwin Yamauchi who has immersed himself in twenty-two languages, ancient archeology, and history says that there is no possibility that the idea of a resurrection was borrowed by Christians from pagans because there is no definitive evidence for the teaching of a deity resurrection in any of the mystery religions prior to the second century. Apparently, the pagans stole the idea of resurrection from the Christians, and not vice-versa.[8]

19. Jesus' resurrection defies any potential alternative explanation. The earliest explanation to disprove Jesus' resurrection was that the body was stolen – which could not have happened with Roman soldiers guarding the body, and still does not explain how the dead body came back to life. Other explanations over the years include that Jesus swooned on the cross, which is impossible without a beating heart, or that everyone who saw Him "alive" suffered from a group hallucination which is impossible because those are private events for one person and not public events for up to five hundred people at a time. Thomas Arnold, former professor of Modern History at Oxford, says, "No one fact in the history of mankind ... is proved by better and fuller evidence of every sort" than the fact that "Christ died and rose from the dead."[9]

The Resurrected Christ Appearing
to the Marys c. 1465
Bartolomeo Rigossi da Gallarate

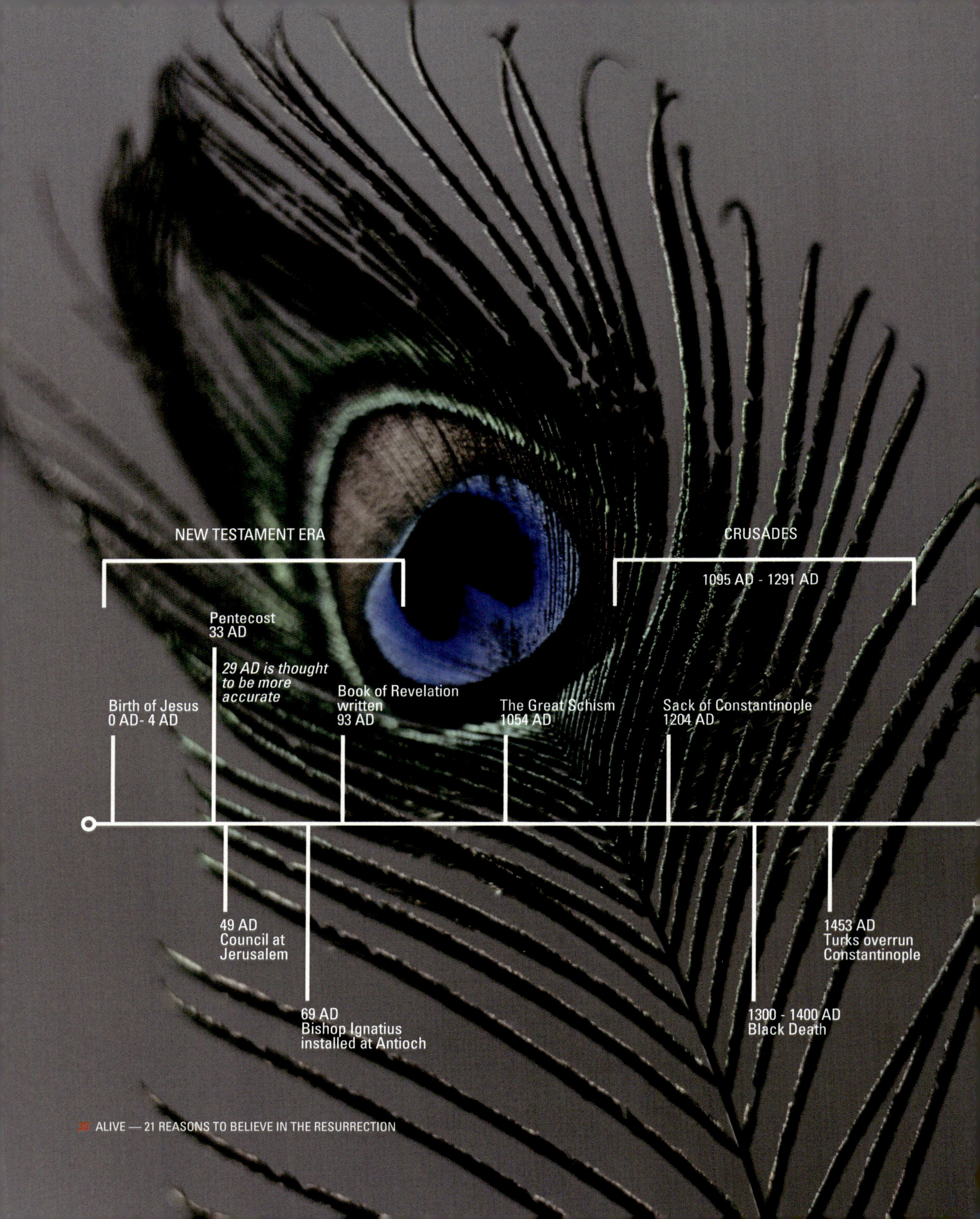
NEW TESTAMENT ERA
CRUSADES
1095 AD - 1291 AD
Pentecost
33 AD
29 AD is thought to be more accurate
Birth of Jesus
0 AD- 4 AD
Book of Revelation written
93 AD
The Great Schism
1054 AD
Sack of Constantinople
1204 AD
49 AD
Council at Jerusalem
69 AD
Bishop Ignatius installed at Antioch
1300 - 1400 AD
Black Death
1453 AD
Turks overrun Constantinople

The peacock is a symbol used by the early church. It loses its beauty during molting, only to have a more beautiful tail appear.

20. Jesus' Church has stood the test of time.
In the wake of Jesus' resurrection, Christianity exploded on the earth and a few billion people today claim to be Christians as the largest, longest lasting, and most diverse movement of any kind on planet earth. The Church of Jesus Christ has not thrived and survived because Christians are smart, organized, or powerful, but only because Jesus Christ is alive and building His Church just like He promised (Matthew 16:18). On this point, C.F.D. Moule of Cambridge University says, "The birth and rapid rise of the Christian Church... remain an unsolved enigma for any historian who refuses to take seriously the only explanation offered by the Church itself."[10]

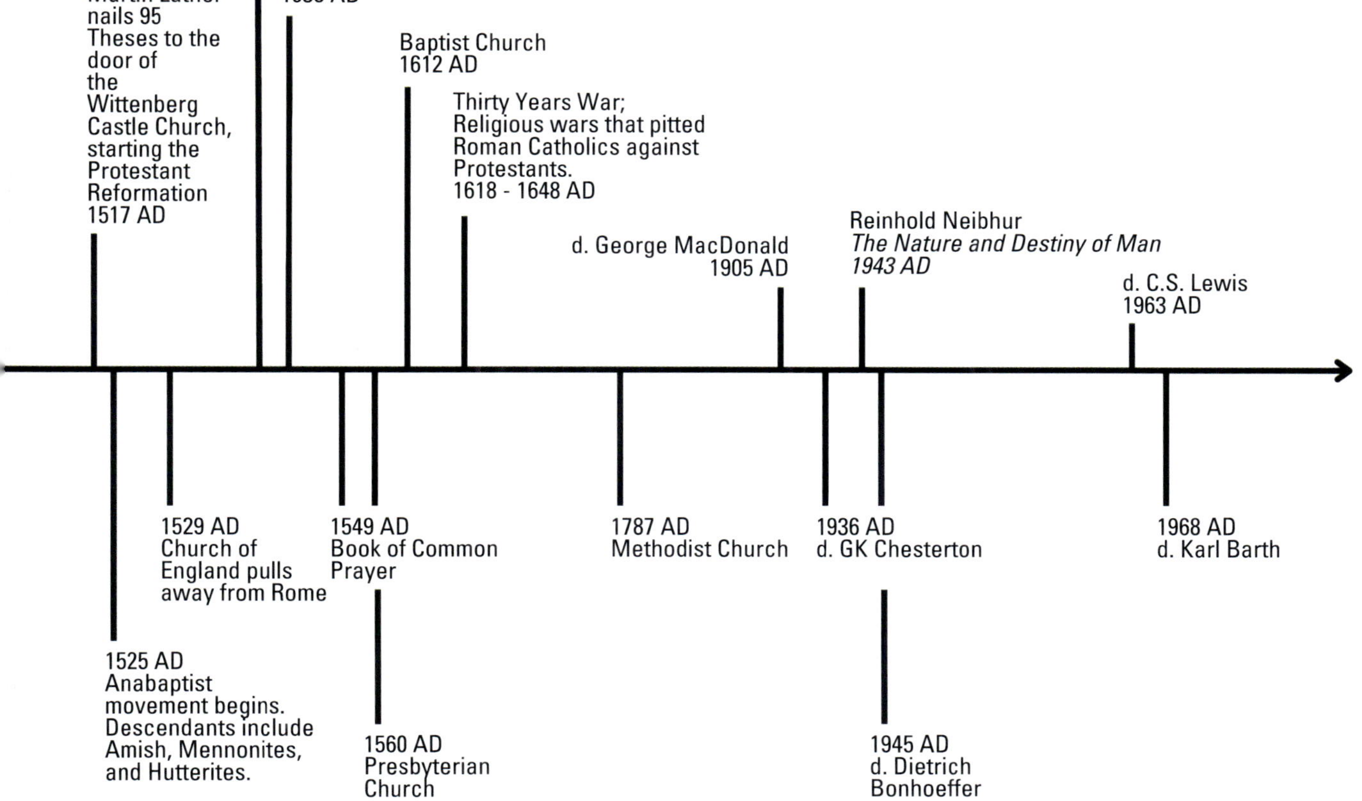

21. Jesus is alive and still changing lives to this day. Throughout life, we reach a lot of conclusions about everything from what car to drive to what food to eat based upon the testimony of friends and family who share their experiences with us. The reason Christians share their testimony about how Jesus changed their life is because they want the people they know and love to come to know the Jesus who loves them. If you know a Christian, ask them about their testimony and you will see that Jesus is alive and still changing lives to this day.

My testimony is that, at the age of 17, a kind pastor's daughter gave me a Bible. At the age of 19, I was reading that Bible and stopped to ask Jesus to forgive my sin and make me a Christian. That day was the most important day of my life, and that decision was the most important one I have ever made. God changed me, along with my desires, and my mind. Without Jesus, nothing in my life would be the same, and everything in my life would be worse. I married the girl who bought me the Bible, and we have been faithfully married to one another since 1992. Today, we have five children. Everyone in our family loves Jesus, seeks to obey the Bible, serves in ministry at the church we started together, feels richly blessed by God and is not afraid of death because we know that Jesus awaits us there. Jesus has changed our lives!

Jesus would love to also change your life and will do so gladly. To start a relationship with Jesus, you need to talk to Him, which is called prayer. Jesus is alive in Heaven and will hear you. You need to apologize to Him for the reason you have not had a relationship with Him—because of your sin which broke that relationship. Then, thank Him for dying on the cross for your sin, and thank Him for raising from the dead for you. Right now, you can be forgiven, loved, made new, and start your eternal relationship with God through Jesus Christ. This eternal relationship with Jesus continues every day of this life and through death into eternity. If you believe in Jesus and belong to Jesus, there is guaranteed eternal life for you. One day your body will rise from death, and you will live as the perfect person God intends for you to be, in a perfected world, filled with joy forever and ever. Jesus loves you, and is waiting to hear from you right now, so ask Him to forgive your sin and change your life!

21

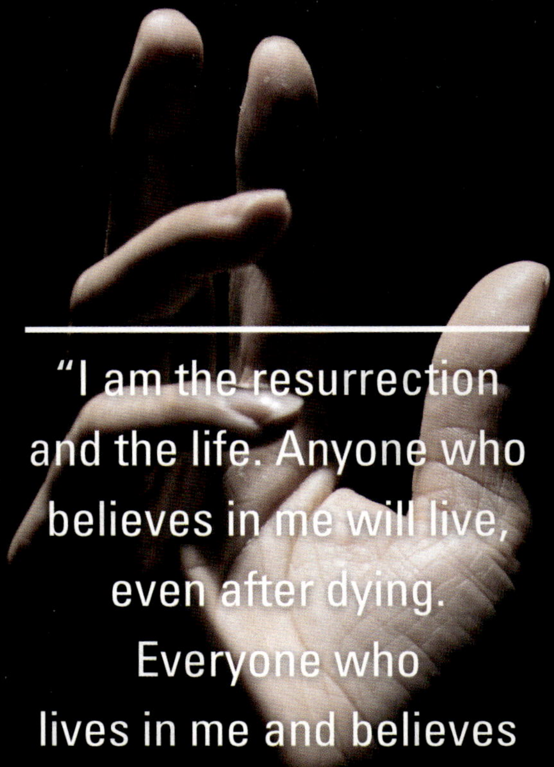

"I am the resurrection and the life. Anyone who believes in me will live, even after dying. Everyone who lives in me and believes in me will never ever die. Do you believe this…?"

JESUS CHRIST
JOHN 11:25–26